Hope & Laughter

PRESENCE BOOKS

EASTBOURNE

Hope and Laughter

Copyright © Mel Compton 2011

The right of Mel Compton to be identified as the author of this work has been asserted by her in accordance with the Copyright, Designs and Patents Act 1988.

All rights reserved.
No part of this publication may be reproduced or transmitted in any form or by any means, electronic or mechanical, including photocopy, recording or any information storage and retrieval system, without permission in writing from the publisher.

Biblical quotations are from the New International Version © 1973, 1978, 1984 by the International Bible Society. Other sources include The New King James Version and the New American Standard translation.

ISBN 978-1-907228-21-6

Published by
PRESENCE BOOKS

Acknowledgements

This book is dedicated to my late Nana, Elsie Cooper who passed away in 2009 having reached an outstanding ninety-six years old. Nana showed me unconditional love and demonstrated to me the power of prayer. I learnt so much from her life and I miss her dearly.

I would like to recognize certain individuals who have greatly impacted my life over the years.

Thank you to Pastors Rob and Julie Smillie and Glenn and Cathy Khan - not only for your excellent teaching but also for your much appreciated support through my life's twists and turns.

Thank you Mum and Dad for bringing me up to know Jesus and to all my family for your perseverance in prayer for restoration in my life. I love you all so much. To Mum and "Little Bro" for your practical help in the editing of "Hope and Laughter".

And of course, to my soul mate, Graham. Not only is he my life partner and an amazing father to our children, but he's also my mentor. No one else could put up with my persistent questions about the Bible!

Most importantly, all glory to God for His never ending goodness and faithfulness to complete what He has begun in our lives.

Mel Compton - May 2011
mel@comptonplace.com

4 Hope and Laughter

Contents

	Foreword	7
1	There's More Than in One in There!	9
2	Hold Onto Your Promise	13
3	Where's Mel?	17
4	Why?	21
5	It's Time	31
6	A Safe Arrival	41
	Pictures	49
7	Back to the Beginning	51
8	Moving On	59
9	My Soul Mate	65
10	The Shared Desire	71
11	A New Year	81
12	The Strongest, Most Beautiful Butterfly	93

6 Hope and Laughter

Foreword

Every woman who has had a baby has a story to tell but this book is so much more than that. I believe that like Melanie you the reader are a unique individual with a God given destiny to fulfil and a unique story all of your own.

As you journey with her she will share her highs and her lows with you. She will hold your hand as you experience this roller coaster we call life and she will speak faith, hope and love into your life whatever your situation.

Her honesty is so refreshing and that's why you will surely find yourself identifying with her. She does not pretend, hide behind a façade of 'super faith' or give you any formulas.

It has been my privilege to be a part of Melanie's journey and to see her relationship with Jesus Christ blossom and grow. Second Corinthians 5:17 says: 'If any person is in Christ the old has passed away. Behold the fresh and new has come.' (Amplified Bible)

Seeing her today as a confident wife, proud Mum, loving daughter, great sister and a wise and supportive friend to many is a true reflection of this precious scripture.

The fact is that most of us have experienced some type of rejection, abuse or hardship or simply made wrong choices that have had consequences for our life. Yes, and sometimes 'stuff' just happens. We can look back down the road of regret or we can look forward and upwards trusting God for the courage to accept the things we cannot change and to change the things we can.

Understanding the 'bigger picture' and that Gods delays are not necessarily his denials, helps us to keep joyful in hope, patient in affliction and faithful in prayer.(Romans12:12)

Holding onto Gods word stabilises us and steadies us in the storms of life. Melanie found it became the sustainer of her soul during the tough times.

Hope resounds through the pages of this book, it lifts and it lights, it perseveres and it promises. Laughter too is healing and a medicine for our souls so smile with her as she recounts those funny moments that life throws unexpectedly our way.

My hope for you dear reader is that as you journey through each chapter fresh faith will fill your heart as you dare to dream and dare to believe in a God who is 'more than able'.

Blessed is the man who trusts in the Lord and has made the Lord his hope and confidence.

Jeremiah 17:7

Pastor Cathy Khan
Sonrise Church

1. There's More Than One in There!

"For I know the plans I have for you, plans to prosper you and not to harm you, to give you a future and a hope" Jeremiah 29:11

Our beautiful twins Hope and Isaac were born on the 26th September 2007 at Portsmouth Hospital, eight weeks before their due date. On the evening of the 24th September my husband Graham prayed earnestly, "Lord, if these babies are okay to be born now, please can it happen soon as Mel is really not coping well!" Some important advice... Be careful what you pray for, because I kid you not, there and then my waters broke!

Graham was right; I really had not been coping well with my pregnancy. It had been bizarre in every sense and had come with the most peculiar and tough symptoms ranging from the normal, yet debilitating sickness, to claustrophobia and panic attacks. Needless to say I had been counting down the days until the arrival! I was ecstatic to be pregnant but was having a very difficult time. I was so excited to be carrying twins, especially the perfect combination of one girl and one boy, but I was quite sure at that point that I never wanted to do pregnancy again!

My pregnancy began with the most severe sickness. For over three months it seemed like I almost permanently had my head in the bucket I had resorted to keeping by my bedside. My skin had taken on a greyish tone and there was no sign of looking "glowing". I had very little energy and seemed to be losing weight rather than gaining it!

10 Hope and Laughter

At about thirteen weeks pregnant the sickness thankfully resided and for a short period of time I felt like I was "glowing", as all the books told me I would be. Now, without the debilitating nausea, I was managing well at my job as a Dispensing Optician and was feeling positive that I would reach my goal of working up to seven months. Life felt great and Graham and I wore permanent smiles on our faces!

Our entire church was celebrating our twin pregnancy with us. Having had quite notable fertility problems our pregnancy was nothing short of an absolute miracle and everyone was so pleased for us.

It was a very memorable day when an early, seven week, scan had revealed not just one heartbeat, but two! Graham and I laughed all the way home! We named our two little miracles that very day. We just had a really strong sense that there would be one boy and one girl.

Some found it strange that we had named them at this point, being so early on in the pregnancy and obviously not yet able to have the sexes determined, but it seemed perfectly normal for us, such was our certainty.

For many years I had believed that at some point in my life, God would give me a little girl and I knew she was to be named Hope. There could only ever be one Hope so we knew our little additional blessing would be a precious boy. Graham and I both loved the name Isaac.

We thought it was trendy yet uncommon enough to be somewhat unique without being weird. What clinched it for us was its meaning......'Laughter!'

Hope and Isaac were our very precious gifts from God for which we were so incredibly grateful. I felt such an awesome sense of honour to be blessed with twins. Having previously been through a difficult stretch in my life, this twin pregnancy was a "literal" fulfilment of Isaiah 61:7 where God promises to restore troubled lives in double measure!

12 Hope and Laughter

2. Hold On to Your Promise

"He will yet fill your mouth with laughter and your lips with shouts of joy" Job 8:21

Following a few weeks of pregnancy ease, a testing time came. During the fourth month I suffered a threatened miscarriage. A hospital scan seemed to show that Hope and Isaac were fine and doctors explained to us that some bleeding could be quite normal, particularly in the case of multiple pregnancies.

I was simply sent home to rest. Doctors said it could go on to be something or nothing; I guess I was sent home really just to see what happened. I remember doing nothing but laying in bed trying to keep any movement to an absolute minimum. I'm sure this had no bearing on the situation but it helped me to think I was doing something I deemed sensible.

Nothing could have prepared me for the love I now felt for Hope and Isaac and I simply could not entertain the idea of losing them. Seeing them during the scans was the most moving experience of my life to that point; last year's seeming impossibilities, now alive and growing within me.

During those days when I was bleeding, Graham and I and our friends and family were praying so hard. Graham remained very strong during this time for which I was really thankful; his faith astounded me and his steadfastness helped me to stay positive.

Faced with a situation of fear Graham was, quite simply, fighting it with faith. I remember him pacing up and down by the bed outwardly declaring God's word and his promises to us. I can't say I felt quite as confident as Graham but I

14 Hope and Laughter

was, to my surprise, more at peace than I would have imagined I would be. It was still a very unpleasant time, a real testing of our faith, but we came through it. After a few days the bleeding stemmed and a scan showed two healthy and strong heartbeats, praise Jesus!

Hope and Isaac are known as "Fraternal Dizygotic" twins. They are a result of two separate eggs, fertilised by two separate sperm. This is opposed to "Monozygotic Identical" twins that result from the fertilisation of one egg and one sperm. Dizygotic twins have the same measure of genetic similarity as any two siblings born to the same parents at different times.

Dizygotic twins demonstrate the strong bond and closeness associated with twins due to them sharing the intrauterine environment from conception through to birth. From around 16 weeks gestation twins can be observed kicking and elbowing each other, fighting for space! It was so fascinating to see both of them during the scans and we quite often observed this vying for space!

It was often difficult for the sonographer to get a good view of either baby as when one baby moved they blocked the view of the other!

I have, over the years, learnt so much from my wonderful husband, the most prominent of which has been about faith. When Graham and I met, he was quite clearly the most grounded in his faith out of the two of us. My husband is naturally a very positive person, a "glass half full" individual. I was, in stark contrast, a "glass half empty" individual. At first I found Graham's constant optimism totally annoying!

When I was fretting about everything and everyone, he was completely calm and it irritated me more than I can express. His lack of worry almost seemed reckless and irresponsible to me.

I soon learnt though that as well as being naturally positive, what my husband had developed over the years was solid trust in God.

Faced with the situation of a potential miscarriage, I had witnessed Graham's faith stir to another level. I could picture him yielding his sword of the spirit, swiping it around in utter defiance, literally fighting fear with faith.

16　Hope and Laughter

3. Where's Mel?

" When I am afraid, I will put my trust in you" Psalm 56:3

Now with everything back on track, just when I thought I might be able to resume enjoying my pregnancy something happened that I could never have anticipated. Very suddenly, I developed anxiety and claustrophobia. There was no warning, one day I woke up and it was just there. Instantly I started to have major panic attacks and they soon began to come regularly.

They first started to occur at work where I started to feel incredibly anxious when my work colleagues and customers were close to me, something that has never bothered me before. I would find myself stepping back to a more comfortable distance. Things snowballed from then on and the anxiety started to creep in to almost every area of my life.

At its worst, I panicked every time someone, other than certain family members, stepped into my personal space. I could not stand anyone coming too close to me and my precious cargo. As you can imagine most situations therefore became difficult. I would really panic.

Fear would flood me within seconds. It was unbearable. I would get all the symptoms associated with panic attacks including the racing heart, the difficulty breathing, and the feeling of lost reality. The best way to accurately describe it is to say I felt I had almost developed a people phobia!

I remember saying to a friend that I was repentant of once mocking someone I had seen on television that had a banana phobia. I had thought how totally ridiculous that was but now I found myself having a rather irrational phobia myself. Since then I have actually watched, with great interest and empathy, a full-length documentary on unusual and life afflicting phobias.

I felt incredibly moved and full of empathy as they documented individuals who were, on a daily basis, plagued by disabling fears of anything ranging from frogs and wind turbines to peas ...yes peas!

Why had I developed such a fear? It was totally irrational, but that is exactly what fear is: irrational, yet very real and frightening to the person experiencing it. At just five months I decided I needed to stop working. I clearly remember the day I walked out of work at the end of the day following seven hours of sheer anxiety.

I knew I would not be going back before the babies were born. I didn't feel I was doing my job properly but most of all I was very concerned about the effects of the high levels of stress on the babies. Being at work became so incredibly traumatic for me it was practically intolerable.

I felt somewhat inadequate having to leave. I had been there over thirteen years and had worked my way up to become the Dispensing Manager of one of the firms' busiest practices. I had always been renowned at my work place for my ability to work well during busy and stressful times.

I took pride in my work and I enjoyed it but with what I was going through I just knew it was time to go. The health of our babies was now my top priority.

Within just weeks I was barely recognisable as the strong confident Melanie I had grown to be during the past few years. I could not understand what was happening to me and I was so frustrated with myself that I could not just snap out of it. I knew what I was experiencing was irrational but I simply could not get round it. I soon found myself avoiding some social settings just to avoid the stress it caused me. It even became difficult for me to have friends over, people I had always loved and trusted. In fact most situations were almost unbearable and I really don't have the words to express how utterly painful and humiliated it made me feel.

It was like the life had been sucked completely out of me. At the end of each day I would collapse in to bed and let the tears flow. I barely remember a night when I did not cry myself to sleep; I can honestly say it was one of the hardest times of my life.

My difficulties obviously affected Graham also. It hurt him to see me this way. In some ways he was powerless to help. He did his best to understand; he prayed and comforted me continually.

I was so relieved that Graham was not a panic trigger for me as that would have been the last straw. I could count the number of people that were not panic triggers to me on just one hand! The entire situation was so utterly bizarre.

Graham was working extra hard to support us following a sudden loss of almost half our income with me having left work well before my maternity pay could kick in. We had also recently moved house and had discovered 101 things that needed doing, preferably before the big arrival!

A keen dinner host, Graham found it very difficult to have a constantly empty house and having to attend many meetings alone. He wanted vivacious Mel back, as did I!

20 Hope and Laughter

4. Why?

"There is surely a future hope for you, and your hope will not be cut off" Proverbs 23:18

I asked God the question "why?" Why was I being subject to so much suffering? I'm sure many will agree, sometimes you simply cannot understand some of the experiences you go through in life. It had been going so well for Graham and I until this point.

We literally had a double portion of God's blessing. In just one year God had healed me of endometriosis, given us a wonderful house and two babies, one for each year of our marriage! It was hard for me to understand how so much blessing could be accompanied by so much difficulty.

Sometimes life can wear us down and overwhelm us to the point where we almost cease to function. Particularly as Christians, we can often find ourselves feeling inadequate and frustrated when we struggle to cope with life's twists and turns.

We often question our faith and wonder why we seem unable to "snap out of it". At these times God is not looking down at us shaking His head in dismay, very much the opposite! God is a God overflowing with compassion. As our creator, God knows and understands all our strengths and our weaknesses.

He knows us inside and out. We were knitted together by His very hands. He knows every word before they leave our lips. He knows the number of hairs on our head. God knows in advance all that we will go through and in every situation He has gone before us. God's hand is always upon us even when we feel He is a million miles away.

Throughout my life I have often experienced God's tangible presence and peace but recently I had a very poignant experience of God's comfort that I will never forget. It was the end of the day and Graham and I were faced with a seemingly impossible situation regarding our finances.

That particular day had been tough on us both and we were both relieved the day was drawing to a close. As I knelt on our lounge floor clearing away the children's building blocks I found myself suddenly quite debilitated by the situation. I stopped what I was doing as I felt the energy drain out of me. I put my head in my hands and lowered my head to the ground.

Moments later, alone in my lounge, I was suddenly aware of Jesus by my side. It was just as though He had come to kneel beside me and gently lay His hand on my back. There was no audible voice, no rushing wind, just an overwhelming sense of peace that flooded me and calmed my inner being as I knelt there with my Father by my side.

God is always our comforter, regardless of how we may be managing, or not managing our emotions throughout difficult times.

I recall a comment a pastor made one day when he said "How much worse could a situation have been if it had not been for God?" This is so true. During my pregnancy, I was especially thankful I had God by my side. I knew without it my experience could well have been much worse.

It is so important that we remain receptive to God during our tough times. It is imperative we keep communicating with Him. Pour out your heart to Him. Scream and shout if you need to; do anything apart from stop communicating with God. My experience is that as you keep communing with Him, you will see that He is providing you with sprinklings of hope via his word, through words of knowledge, through others' love and support and through what Graham and I refer to as "God-incidences". As long as you allow Him, God will never fail to give you all you need to keep going.

Whilst I did not understand all that was happening one thing that was clear to me was that God was constantly throwing me lifelines that were keeping me afloat. Yes, daily life was at times nothing short of traumatic for me, but every day I got out of bed, got dressed and persevered!

If you find you are still able to do this in a time of difficulty be encouraged, you are "afloat". The very act of you getting out of bed means there is still that God-given hope within you.....cling to that hope as you would cling to the ropes attached to a parachute if you were falling through the sky!

One main stream of encouragement came via a dear friend in the early stages of my anxiety. Unaware of the degree to which I was suffering God had given her an encouraging word for me. She said that God could see what I was going through but that I was not to fear as God had his protective hand over me.

These experiences were bruising me but that was as far as it could go. This really spoke to me because what happens with a bruise? It fades; it's superficial, the pain soon passes and after time there is no remaining evidence of the bruise whatsoever!

I was so thankful for this encouragement. It became one of my "cling-ons" as I kept on walking through this period of my life.

I firmly believe that God gave me a very specific rhema word for this season of my life when one evening I opened my Bible and a passage simply jumped out at me. Whilst it is not always advisable to play "Russian roulette" with your

Bible, I believe quite often, especially in desperate situations, God in his goodness and grace will meet your need this way.

God did that very thing with me that evening. It simply read: "It will not happen in that which you think". The book, chapter and verse are irrelevant. In fact if I read the entire verse of which those few words were a part, it would have made no sense at all, thus confirming even more strongly that those few words were exactly what God wanted me to read, nothing more, nothing less.

For me that was the calming of the storm. These words were my hope, my anchor. Those few words were the exact words I needed, as at times I would find my mind imagining the worst. In all honesty I had come to feel that I was heading for a complete nervous breakdown.

I often found myself thinking "What if this, what if that?". My mind would go through every possible situation imaginable! This rhema word was one of the fundamental encouragements I needed during this time.

I once saw a tiny spider dangling from its thread in my bathroom. When you see spiders like this it looks like they are simply hanging in mid air. Only when you look very closely can you see their thread. The spider was fine, he had his support but only when I inspected very closely could I see it.

Sometimes when we feel afraid and feel almost like God has left us, we need to look a little closer to see that God is in fact holding on to us. His lifeline is always there, we just need to open our eyes wider to realise it.

If anything had caused the thread to break, the spider would quickly spin another. In the same way, whenever we feel horribly vulnerable and detached, God throws us another lifeline. He is always there ahead of us. At the moment of difficulty He is in front making a way.

Romans 4:16 talks of God re-kindling our faith when we have run out of hope. Significantly God re-named Abraham to "Abram" meaning the "Father of all Nations" **before** Abram bore Isaac. This re-kindled Abram's faith, at a time when he was running out of hope.

Despite the fact that much time had passed and he was ageing; this change of name enabled him to keep hold of God's promise to him that he would bear a son. God had thrown him a lifeline.

Through all of this I decided I would do my best to maintain a positive attitude. I managed better on some days than others! I was kind to myself and set myself small but manageable targets to reach each day. A trip to the local shopping centre was a big achievement.

Even if I could only manage a short time, I congratulated myself and encouraged myself that next time I would be able to spend more time there.

Despite the process of becoming pregnant and being pregnant not being anything like I had imagined or hoped, it still remained an amazing miraculous event to happen in my life and as such I wanted to document it from start to finish.

My journal became a daily routine that really helped me sift through my thoughts, hand each day to God and clear my mind in preparation for what was to come next.

I intricately detailed each day, often giving a graphic description of all my pregnancy related issues. In the more fragile times of my pregnancy I used my journal to pour out my feelings to God, my words becoming my prayers; my soul crying out to God to move.

At the end of each day, writing my journal was a way for me to offload in a depth that I could not do to anyone else around me. This personal documentation was so beneficial to me. It was like I was saying to the Lord, "This has been my day, I give it to you, please renew my strength for tomorrow." My journal would make a very interesting read. However, to this day, it remains completely private between me, the paper it is written on and, of course, God!

As you can imagine, continuing to go to a people filled church was of course a tough one for me during this time, but it was one thing I knew I must try my best to continue with. When you least want to go is when you most need to go!

You hear that so often but it is so very true. I found that if I sat mid row with people around me on each side that was a panic trigger. My solution, rather than to miss church, was to sit front row at the end with Graham to the side. We developed a strategy by which if I reached for his hand he knew I was starting to panic and he would put his arm round me and pray quietly for me.

For most situations I developed self-help strategies. I'm sure anyone reading this who has suffered with anxiety would relate to this. One of the things I found helped me, quite bizarrely, was to be holding on to something, whether it be my bag or even just a tissue. Graham's hand was my preferred choice but sadly not always available!

The saddest thing about my dilemma was my seeming inability to be around my dearest friends. I have many dear friends and it so upset me that I was finding it nearly impossible to stay for fellowship following services.

Normally Graham and I would be some of the last to leave and now I was dragging him out the door as quickly as I could. Friends so wanted to help me but really all they could do was pray. As I took myself off the social circuit I wondered how my friendships would survive.

One unforgettable moment was when one of my close friends approached me following the service. I was still in my seat, the service only just that moment finished. All that this person wanted to do was to hug me and show their support and within seconds of us greeting I had made an excuse of needing the toilet and fled! I was devastated, absolutely devastated.

I knew this individual would think nothing less of me but still I felt awful. It felt so frustrating that the one thing I so needed, friendship and support, was the one thing the very nature of my problem was affecting. I had heard about the flight or fight responses that people have as a natural way of dealing with situations of fear, and I realised I was starting to take "flight" in almost every one to one situation.

The anxiety seemed to be worsening as the time went on. Another significantly hard time for me was when it came to our yearly church conference held in Brighton. I desperately wanted to attend, we had already booked and they are always awesome events.

Hundreds of people come from nations all over the world to our yearly conferences so it was unlikely that I would be able to get my 'on the end, no-one around me seat'! To my amazement I still went and managed to sit through most of the sessions.

I clung to Graham's arm most of the time. I admit I could not recall all that was preached but I was glad I went. I was able to soak up God's presence if nothing else. I was really pleased to discover that everything was broadcast into the toilets!

This was great because each time the panic started to overwhelm me I would go and sit on the toilet to calm down and would not completely miss out! In the circumstances I had found myself in I was determined not to be utterly defeated; my determination a result of the hope still within me.

There is a very inspiring story about an old, tired and worn out donkey who had been thrown down a well by his owner. In an attempt to kill him the owner then proceeded to throw buckets full of dirt on top of the donkey. The donkey, desperate to survive, used this falling dirt to his advantage. With each bucket load of dirt that fell on his head, the donkey shook it off and trampled it under foot. The more dirt that came at him, the more he trampled it beneath his feet.

Before long, he had trampled down so much dirt that he came completely up out of the well! Praise God and thank God for the donkey! The moral of the story obviously being that whatever satan is throwing at you, refuse to give up.

Refuse! God always gives you all the daily strength you need to fight the enemy. Never stop trusting God and keep persevering. By going to this conference, even if I had to listen to the speakers whilst sitting on the toilet, this was my way of persevering, my way of trampling on the dirt. I was determined to rise up out of the well.

I did speak to my doctor about my difficulties, but found myself giving him a slightly watered down version of it all. I guess, like many pregnant or post pregnant women I was reluctant to explain how bad it was in case he thought I would not be able to cope post birth.

He was very understanding and explained that what I was experiencing was not unheard of, particularly in those women who had been through high level hormone treatment and had a multiple pregnancy like me. I was proving very sensitive to the extreme levels of hormones, both those associated with the pregnancy, plus all the hormones given as part of the fertility process I had had to aid my conception.

He felt I had developed anti-natal depression and the anxiety was perhaps a symptom of this. I had never heard of anti-natal depression, only post, but I now understand it is a recognised condition and affects many women.

A few years prior to this I had suffered a bout of anxiety, not to the same degree however. This had been partly attributed to some hormone treatment I had been on at that time and so it seemed perhaps I had a predisposition to it, particularly when there was an upset to my hormone balance.

Generally speaking though, to try to analyse why something is happening has little benefit. It normally serves only to magnify the concern! Whatever the reason for this happening to me, it was what I was faced with and I just had to keep walking.

My doctor explained to me that medication was available to reduce the anxiety but not without risk to the babies so, as far as I was concerned, it was a total no-go. I was also offered counselling but I decided against this rightly or wrongly. It may possibly have helped but even the thought of being shut in a small room talking to a stranger stressed me!

It was a bit of a 'catch 22' situation. I'm not at all averse to counselling and I believe it can be hugely beneficial but in this case I opted against it.

My doctor encouraged me that it was all quite clearly pregnancy related and would, no doubt, dispel after the birth. To hear him say this, was in itself, a big help. Funnily enough, another most helpful comment was one I received from a dear friend, a lady who is now my pastor.

Her initial reaction to what I was going through was, "That does not sound like the Mel I know!" Exactly, I was not the Mel I knew also! But she would be back. I just had to keep going; keep walking though the valley until I came out the other end. And that is exactly what I did!

30 Hope and Laughter

5. It's time!

" He is before all things, and in him all things hold together" Colossians 1:17

On the evening of the 24th September 2007, I sat uncomfortably on a sofa in our church function room. Graham and I were at our weekly Bible school lesson. We were both undertaking a two year course held once a week run by our church. I was so pleased that I had managed to continue with the majority of it during my pregnancy. The more disturbing my situation became, the keener I was to spend time in the word renewing my mind.

The main group was sat to my right in the usual classroom-like table arrangement. Fortunately I had been able to sit on the comfier sofas on my own during the latter stages of my pregnancy. Not only was this more comfortable for me but it enabled me to have a fighting chance of actually staying put! As I sat there I started to feel extremely hot, like someone had set me alight from the inside.

The theory of spontaneous human combustion came to mind. I felt extremely ill and more than usually irritated. At seven months pregnant with twins I felt like my abdomen would explode. No position was comfortable. It was still hot even in late September and I was struggling physically as well as emotionally.

At twenty-two weeks the sonographer had confirmed I was carrying one girl and one boy. Graham and I had simply grinned at each other! I think if Graham and I are completely honest, we felt slightly "smug" as we confirmed with friends the sexes of our children. We had known right from the start we would have the perfect combo!

Now our precious Isaac was on the left, head up, directly under my rib cage, restricting my breathing somewhat! Hope was on the right, her head now lodged in my pelvis! I was totally in love with my children and was so proud to be carrying them but I really wondered how I was going to cope as they had their last minute growth spurt!

I already had quite considerable discomfort in various parts of my body. There was an almost constant pain in my bladder region and every breath I took was quite strained and tight. My rib cage had quite clearly moved, as if the ribs were opening up each side, an oddity that has remained the same post birth. There was also a recurring sharp pain at the base of my spine.

I was managing to get comfy in bed thankfully but to get out of bed on my own was now nearly impossible and I was reliant on Graham to be my hoist.

I wondered how, in these final weeks, I would move. How would I fit any food in my stomach? During the last two weeks before this point I had started being sick again in the mornings....the joy! I had a feeling the birth would be earlier rather than later. I had been advised to expect an early delivery with twins.

We were ready. My bags were packed. The nursery was already decorated - beautifully by Graham. Our friends had blessed us with all we could possibly want for the babies. The car seats were ready and waiting and I had packed all the relevant necessities for what I assumed would be a short hospital stay. I had my nursing pads and disposable pants ready!

During that Monday evening at Bible school I somehow managed to bear how I was feeling and remain until the end. On closing I went to the ladies and noticed my face was beetroot red. Before making our way home I joked with friends that I felt the birth was imminent but I had no idea how imminent!

That evening a friend had given us two boxes of baby clothes and after returning from Bible school, feeling a little less hot by this stage, I sat on the lounge floor excitedly sorting through the clothes.

At about 11.00 p.m. Graham and I went to bed. I explained to Graham how poorly I had felt during the evening. It had been hard for Graham to see me go through all I had that year so far. The fertility treatment had been tough on me, as had the entire pregnancy. In desperation he called out to God asking for the early birth of our babies. Of course we only wanted this if the babies would be okay.

Then, oh my word, God answered Graham's prayer! Instantly my waters broke! Nobody had warned me what waters breaking was like! Obviously, I had more water to come out having twins but even still… my word! At first I thought I had wet the bed and remember actually telling Graham as such!

It soon, however, became apparent what was actually happening! Within seconds the bed was flooded! I was beside myself! "It's time!" I yelled to Graham. I expected him to be really calm at this time but he seemed to just forget exactly what he needed to do! "Get dressed" he kept repeating to me but with every pair of pants and trousers I put on, I flooded straight through them!

At this point Graham was attempting to strip the bed sheets! Priorities! "Phone the hospital," I yelled! They advised us to come straight away but it must have been a good half hour later when we arrived! When I finally stopped gushing everywhere I was able to put some clothes on and stay dry. I also had to phone my parents and my brother to tell them the news.

Everyone at the other end of the phone was very excited, although I could tell they were a little concerned. Mum prayed for me over the phone. She knew I was scared, as any first time mum must be before they give birth. I did not know what lay ahead and I have always had a very low pain threshold so knew I was going to be really wimpy about the entire thing!

At this point, however, I was shaking like crazy but was not in any pain. Although my waters had broken there was no sign of any contractions so I did not feel the need to hurry. I would not leave until I had checked my hair and applied my lippy! I am never seen without my pink lippy and this was not going to be any exception!

When we arrived at the hospital I felt strangely calm. We even bumped into a friend of ours. "Why are you here?" He asked, "Oh, I'm just having the babies," I answered! It was very surreal and not how I pictured it to be. Not like in the movies where the couple rush in to the hospital and the man is shouting: "Quick, my wife is having a baby!" And the woman bent over yelling, barely able to walk!

In stark comparison, Graham and I were slowly making our way through the empty corridors of Eastbourne Hospital to the delivery suite. I chuckled to myself as I remembered that we were soon due to have a delivery suite tour as part of our anti-natal classes. I was having our babies well before my classes had even finished! The midwife who, in fact, headed up the classes greeted us at the delivery suite door. She looked quite shocked as she knew that I was still a long way from my delivery date.

I think at this point it did dawn on me how premature this was. I was only thirty-two weeks and the last scan we had had a few weeks prior suggested the babies were not even 3lb each yet. I remember thinking how tiny our babies would be but I tried not to let my mind wander any further than that. God was taking care of them and me so all would be fine.

Graham and I then had a big shock when we were then informed that I would need to be transferred to another hospital. At just thirty-two weeks, it was assumed our babies would need some form of special care and the special care baby unit was full!

I had never imagined this scenario! Graham and I were left in a room overnight whilst the staff tried to find somewhere to take me. By this stage I was developing small light contractions about an hour apart but was not showing signs of imminent labour. A midwife would pop in every few hours to check on me. I was hooked up to a baby monitor to check the babies were fine. As the babies were no longer in their protective water I was started on a course of antibiotics to prevent the risk of infection. I had automatically assumed that labour would start directly after the waters had broken but apparently this is not always the case. It could be days or even weeks before the next stage started. Had it not been for the mild pain I had started experiencing I would have been sent home again.

By the early hours of the morning I was feeling a little stressed. I hated the idea of being sent elsewhere away from my familiar surroundings. The hospital in Hastings, which is just a half hour away, did not take any mothers under 34 weeks gestation so that ruled me out.

We then found out that I was to be sent to Portsmouth, which is about two hours drive away, and mid morning on the 25th September I was transported by ambulance to Portsmouth Hospital, Graham following behind in our car. The journey seemed to take forever. I felt de-hydrated and there was only one small strange little tub of water for me to drink the entire journey.

As I lay there during the journey I closed my eyes and drifted in and out of sleep. I started to find myself really calling out to God for his strength to help me deal with the hours ahead. At this point my anxiety was still rife so not only was I having to deal with the impending birth but also the necessity of constant close medical attention. I was starting to feel very nervous.

I felt a little better when we arrived and I was re-united with Graham. We had a lovely big room to ourselves with views across Portsmouth. The midwives were wonderful, very gentle and reassuring yet I was still most uncomfortable having them constantly leaning directly over me with their scanners and monitors. I could not take flight in this situation!

Every time they came in to the room to tend to me I took a deep breath and tried desperately to remain as calm as possible. It did not even cross my mind to tell them of the anxiety issue; what was the point? They needed to do their job and look after all three of us. Outwardly I probably appeared like any other first time mum pre birth but on the inside I was frantically calling out to God as my nerves reached an all time high.

At this point my contractions were still mild and very far apart and in fact what they tried to do first was stave off my labour with some medication. They wanted to try to delay labour to enable them to have time to inject me with a course of steroids to strengthen the babies' lungs.

They were quite sure it would be days before I would deliver and so early evening they put up a bed beside mine for Graham and we both tried to settle down for some much needed sleep.

All throughout my pregnancy I had had to inject myself daily with a blood thinning drug as I have Factor 5 Leiden, a blood disorder that gives me an elevated risk of blood clots, particularly during pregnancy. I really hated these injections and cringed every time I did it. I had to learn to inject myself during my fertility treatment so you would imagine that seven months down the line I would be taking it in my stride but not so!

I made Graham laugh as I always felt the need to do a funny little dance of relief around the room after each time I had plunged the needle in my tummy!   Later on that evening a midwife came in to give me my daily blood thinning injection. Little did I know how much trouble that single injection would cause just a short while after.

As I lay in a strange room, in a strange hospital, in a strange town I felt so thankful my husband was asleep at my side. I had that funny feeling of butterflies in my tummy and was almost constantly shaking from head to toe. I just wanted it all to be over and have my babies in my arms. I had heard so many birthing stories, some good, some dreadful!

My mum had had what I can only describe as a supernatural birth with me. She literally had just a few moderate contractions and then I popped out! She had found the whole experience totally bearable, almost enjoyable! However I had imagined this time to be, I knew it would be totally different!   I was right. For a start, I was not in the hospital I had thought I would be in!

As the hours went by I started to wonder whether the labour delaying pills were working! I was sure my contractions were strengthening and drawing closer. I mentioned this to the midwife and she responded by giving me another tablet! The contractions felt like very bad period pains. I managed to cope with about three contractions on my own by curling up in to a ball with each one but then finally, as the pain progressed, I decided I ought to wake Graham who was sound asleep at my side.

He had not slept in 48 hours and was shattered, so shattered that it was difficult to wake him up. "I think it is happening" I kept saying, but bless him; he just did not want to get up! He was obviously in one of those really deep sleeps, the ones where, when you stir, you feel like a dead weight and completely lifeless. "I need sleep," he murmured!

I'm sure for a moment he had forgotten where we were and what was happening! I on the other hand had not, and as I had another, increasingly painful and by this stage quite distressing, contraction I became cross! "Get up Graham; I am not doing this on my own!"

The pills had not worked! Quite the opposite! Contrary to what the doctors had thought, I was going to have our babies that night, not in a few days! Labour had come on very quickly and an excruciating internal examination revealed I was almost six cm dilated and Hope was on her way out! I was scared, really scared. I was now shaking uncontrollably.

The doctors explained to me that because they had only given me my blood thinning drug a few hours before, they would be unable to give me an epidural to aid a natural delivery. If I had an epidural I would almost definitely have a severe bleed. Having twins naturally without an epidural could be very traumatic for me and potentially quite a risk for all of us.

Basically, giving me my blood thinning injection that night had been a big mistake! There was only one option for me and that was a C-section under general anaesthetic. Not the way they usually like to do them. Graham and I tried to take it all in as the doctor explained the risks for me.

Because I had recently eaten there were risks of me being sick during and after the operation. There was also, for a reason I forget, a risk of my throat closing up and they explained they would need to put a tube down my throat to

keep the airway open. Just to top all of that, there was also the risk of infection and bleeding after the operation. What choice did we have? There was no other way of getting the children out safely!
Within ten minutes I was making my way down the corridor to theatre, having a contraction as I walked. I had another as I lay on the theatre table whilst they prepped me. It really was a nasty experience. There were medical staff all around me, all seemingly doing something different.

Some were inserting needles, another a catheter. I clearly remember one nurse frantically pulling my hair band out for some reason taking some hair with it! It was obvious everyone was in a hurry and time was of the essence.

I felt like a piece of meat being prodded and pulled about and I was in excruciating agony. But I knew they were doing all they needed to do for all three of us. It's true what they say, you lose all dignity but you simply don't care!

I panicked as they held the mask over my face to put me to sleep. The worst bit was that for some reason they had to push down on my throat. That part was horrific but thankfully I was not aware of it for more than a few seconds then I was gone. If I'm honest there were moments when I had wondered whether I was going to be with Jesus!

Graham and I had had a brief opportunity to pray together privately just before I went to surgery. We stood together; held hands and prayed earnestly for a safe delivery. I had wanted Graham with me all the way, but at the theatre doors we had to say goodbye.
Bless him, he was anxious too. This was equally hard for him and he was aware, like me, that the situation had, very quickly, become very serious. My life and the babies had become at risk. It was a comfort to know all the time I was in theatre Graham would be deep in prayer, and for that I was so grateful.

Hope and Laughter

6. A Safe Arrival.

"May he grant you according to your heart's desire and fulfil all your purpose" Psalm 20:4

As I slowly came round from the anaesthetic I felt a surge of joy within me at the realisation that I was now a proud mum of twins. There was no doubt as to whether the babies were okay as I had an inner assurance all was well.

I began to become aware of Graham's voice and him holding my hand. "The babies are fine, they are beautiful" he said. Sadly I did not experience being handed my babies directly after the birth. The doctors had briefly brought Hope and Isaac to show Graham before they were transported directly to the special care unit.

He had not been allowed to hold them or even touch them. It had previously been explained to us that this would be the case. Due to their prematurity it was important that they were promptly put into warm incubators where they would continue their growth in a womb like environment.

A nurse brought me two beautiful photos of Hope and Isaac taken directly after their birth. I could hardly take it in as I looked at them, they were beyond description, their eyes were closed and they looked so calm. Hope had a mass of dark hair; Isaac, in stark comparison, had very fine blonde hair. They looked so incredibly tiny.

They had tiny little knitted hats on, the size you would put on a child's dolly or teddy. I was blown away by the feelings I had towards them and this was before I had seen them in the flesh. They were our little miracles, seven months ago microscopic embryos, now little babies for us to nurture and love.

I later learnt that the actual birth had been quite traumatic so I was pleased that I had been totally unaware! Hope was lodged in the birthing canal and had had to be quite forcibly pulled out in the opposite direction. She was born first at 1.36 a.m.

Isaac had then been very quickly delivered just one minute after his big sister. Both children had apparently cried instantly after delivery, a very good sign. They were small but not as small as they could have been at just 32 weeks. Isaac was the heaviest at 3 lb 9 ounces and Hope was just a fraction smaller at 3 lb 6 ounces. Isaac needed some oxygen at first but soon was managing on his own. Hope was breathing well, on her own, but it was explained to us that her head was badly bruised from the delivery. She was also jaundiced.

Graham was obviously so relieved I was okay. Lying still I was not in much pain, but I did wonder how I would sit up. I tried not to imagine what they had had to do to me to get the babies out, especially as they had been in a hurry. The thought made me cringe. I had heard so many horror stories about recovery from C-sections and how you could not do anything for weeks! One friend had talked of a need to hold her lower tummy in all the time as it felt like all would spill out!

At that particular point in time all I cared about was meeting our babies. The doctors wanted me to rest until morning and have some breakfast before I could be taken to see them. Morning soon came and a nurse helped me to get out of bed and into a wheel chair. Sitting up was agony, and yes I did feel the need to hold on to my lower tummy! It's true girls …. hold that tummy tight otherwise you may lose everything!

I was unbelievably excited as Graham wheeled me down to the special care unit. This was to be the most moving, most desired moment of my entire life. For ten years I had longed to be a mum, now the wait was finally over and I was about to meet the dear children I had carried and cherished for the last seven months. Portsmouth special care baby unit is one of the biggest in the country; it was a mass of incubators, tubes and equipment.

Most parents either were sat or stood by their babies peering helplessly into the incubators. The situation was not as I imagined it. I longed to have my babies in my room with me like other mums.

Before I had given birth, one of the neonatal nurses had come to visit Graham and I to explain to us what to expect from the special care unit. We had been shocked to discover that we would have to be prepared for our babies to possibly be in special care until term before we could take them home.

If they did well and gained weight quickly it could be sooner. Neither one of us had thought of this. We had just assumed we may be in hospital for a week then we would all go home. Not only had my pregnancy not been how I had expected but now my post birth experience was about to be not how I had imagined it.

I had to be careful not to dwell on that side of things; I had to be grateful our babies had been safely delivered. I wanted them to have the best start in life they could, and if this meant being specially cared for in hospital for a couple of months then I knew God would carry us through that time.

Our babies were at first in separate rooms. We were taken to see Isaac first. As I set eyes on him my entire body filled with warmth and maternal love raced all through me. He looked so helpless and vulnerable. He was on his tummy, his head on one side. His limbs were thin and the skin on his bones was wrinkled for lack of fat. He simply wore a nappy. The nappy swamped him; it came right up to his chest. There was a tube going to his tummy via his mouth to feed him with small amounts of my breast milk.

I desperately wanted to hold him to comfort him. The frustration at not being able to do so was immense. Tears flooded down my face. I felt a mixture of delight and sadness. I wondered how he was feeling, did he feel okay, or was he in pain?

I comforted myself in that he looked so peaceful. He was fast asleep and was lovely and warm. I wondered if he knew he had been born. Did he know he was no longer in my tummy? All these thoughts ran through my mind. Graham and I were so moved.

Graham and I had a son together and he was amazing. We were not allowed to hold him at this point but we were able to put our hands through the incubator holes and lay them gently on Isaac. The nurses explained that any sudden movement would disturb him. The incubators job was basically to replicate the womb like environment whilst Isaac continued his growth and development. A blanket had even been rolled up and placed around his feet. This was to make him feel secure - as in the womb.

As we touched him, the feelings of love grew deeper still. His skin was unbelievably soft and beautifully warm. Our hearts jumped as he stretched out his leg. This time I was watching him move rather than feel him move. He was perfect!

After some time with Isaac we were taken to see Hope. The same maternal warmth fled through me yet again. This time, however, it was accompanied by a deeper sadness. As I looked closely I saw that her head was indeed extremely bruised and somewhat misshapen. She certainly had had a bumpy arrival. Her eyelids and face were slightly swollen. She too was very thin.

A Safe Arrival   45

Her hands were exceptionally tiny. Again I desperately wanted to hold her and not let go. Despite the bumps and bruises we were assured she was okay. Like Isaac she looked peaceful which was a comfort to us. We watched as she slept and touched her warm skin as we had done with Isaac. I knew from that moment that my life had changed. I was now a mummy to the two most precious babies in the world.

I felt a different woman, I felt fulfilled in every sense.   In front of my very eyes was last year's impossibility. I knew that there would not be a day go by when I would not thank God for them.

God is so gracious. As our Father, He longs to shower us with good gifts just as we do with our children. God had known the deep desires of my heart; He had heard my heartfelt prayers as I cried out to Him on bended knee. God had now blessed me above and beyond that which I could have ever expected. What had I done to deserve this? Nothing!

The Bible says our best efforts at being righteous are but dirty rags! But God knows our hearts. I had sought God diligently and clung to His word. There had been times, however, when I found myself on my bedroom floor wrenched over in physical anguish as I wondered how much longer I could go without bearing a child.

There were times when it was all I could think about and there were times when I felt I was losing all faith. But each time I found myself like this I picked myself up, got right with God and carried on in his strength.   I refused to give up hope and dared to believe the day would come when I would become a mum.

I recall being on the bus on my way in to work one day, a year or so before I fell pregnant. As I thought about my desire to be a mum I said to myself "Dare to believe Mel, dare to believe". God is no respecter of status. I knew God was a God of miracles and I had chosen to believe that He would provide Graham and I with the miracle we so desired. Now these miracles lay before us, Hope Esther and Isaac Fraser, permanent reminders of God's goodness to us.

Hope and Isaac remained in Special Care for one month, the first week at Portsmouth, then a further three weeks in Eastbourne Special Care Unit. Having your new born babies in special care when the majority of the mums in your ward are taking their babies home within just days is both frustrating and emotional.

There are no cots by your bedside, just a breast pump! There is no immediate opportunity for breastfeeding bonding time as you have to wait for your precious ones to grow before they are strong enough to feed that way. Hours were spent each day expressing milk that was refrigerator stored and fed to Hope and Isaac via tubes.

It was a surreal experience, loaded with an emotional high but yet tinged with an unsettling feeling. In the early days of their special care every day was spent spending as much time by their incubators as we were allowed, just watching and praying. We stood back as nurses regularly came to attend and check on them. There were so many wires and tubes and bleeping noises. There was such a sense of helplessness on our part. They looked so vulnerable. I recall the first time they opened their eyes, it was so very moving, beyond description.

When they were a few days old we were allowed to begin holding them, just for short periods of time at first. Graham and I would be sat next to each other, each with a child in our arms and we would be completely silent, usually with tears in our eyes! We could have stayed like it for hours but within a short space of time, the nurses would come in and place our dear children back in their warm incubators.

A Safe Arrival 47

A very significant time came for me when the children were moved to Eastbourne Special Care Unit. We arrived late at night, the children having been transported via ambulance with Graham and I following behind in our car. We were welcomed by the Eastbourne night staff and taken to the rooms that would be homes for Hope and Isaac for the next few weeks. They were in separate rooms at first, rooms that were barely big enough to house the incubators themselves. As I suddenly found myself in one of these tiny rooms with Graham and two staff nurses I inwardly called out to God, " Lord this anxiety has to leave me NOW, there is no option now. Lord, it has to GO!".

From that very point it quite quickly stopped being an issue. Within a matter of days I noticed I was hardly having to contend with it at all. I felt, at times, very emotional and overwhelmed but as far as the claustrophobia and "people" phobia I really sensed that it was, at last, behind me.

There was no way I could have survived the weeks ahead in that small special care unit otherwise. I'm sure the sudden hormonal shift post birth had played a part as well but I really sensed God's hand in it and I was really thankful I did not have to deal with it alongside my first weeks as a new mum.

With each day in special care, although tough, I kept strong, knowing that with each passing day I was a day nearer to taking them home. It was a challenging time as there was a strict regime of feeding, dressing, nappy changing, washing and expressing milk,. No sooner was it done for one child, before it was needed for the other. I was given a printed timetable to work to!

It was exhausting but very good preparation for when I took Hope and Isaac home! With Graham now back at work my mum came in to hospital every weekday to help me. Mum was amazing and I was so thankful for her support. Mum drove 45minutes each morning from her home to take me to the hospital first thing in the morning and she would stay with me the entire day. All our family and friends fell instantly in love with our new additions and it was so touching to watch peoples' faces brim with emotion as they met the children for the first time.

There were a few complications with Hope and Isaac's health in the early days. Hope developed a bleed within her brain most probably due to her traumatic delivery. Fortunately scans showed the bleeding stem and now nearly three years on her perfectly normal development shows there was no permanent damage done.

She was also very jaundiced in the early stages but this I understand can be very common. She actually looked very sweet yellow! Isaac gave us a few frights with regards to needing oxygen occasionally but as each day went by his lungs became stronger and he began to manage just fine.

All in all *Special Care* was tough yet a necessary time through which Graham and I were so strongly aware of Gods protective hand. The day we finally walked out of hospital with Hope and Isaac in their carrier chairs we were full of both unbelievable joy and an intriguing anticipation of how radically different our lives would be from that point.

The Big Day

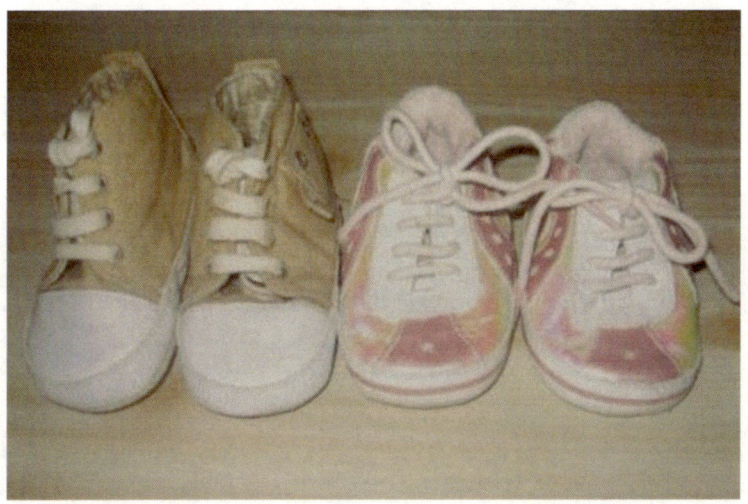

The Faith Shoes

50 Hope and Laughter

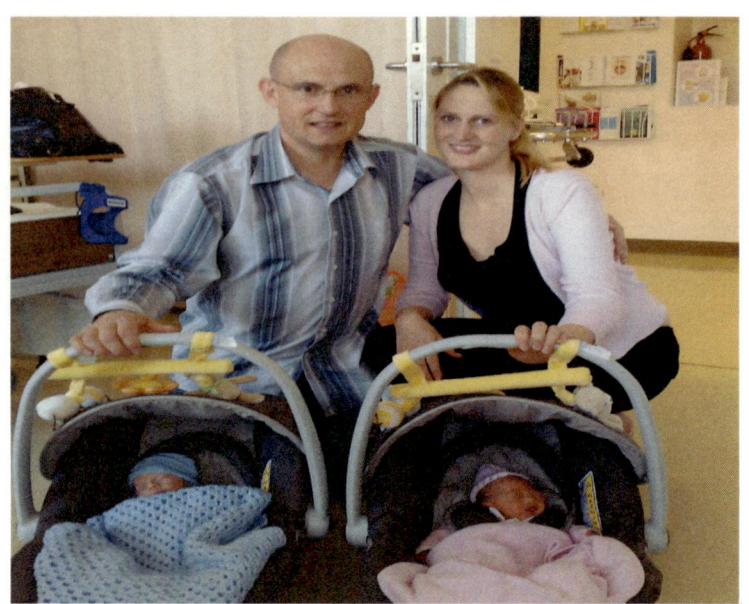

The Miracle Babies – Homeward Bound

Laughter and Hope – Isaac and Hope

7. Back to the Beginning

" I will not fail you or forsake you" Joshua 1: 5

As I looked at my precious little girl I thought how much the name suited her. It was just perfect. Unusual without being strange as some names are today! Although born in 2007, Hope's story actually began almost a decade before.

I was raised in a wonderful Christian home and I gave my life to Jesus at just 7 years of age and was baptised at 13. I knew what it was to love God and understood my salvation but looking back I realise I was not as immersed in my faith as I could have been.

Sadly, as a teenager I walked away from God, foolishly thinking I could do life without him and that I could create my own happiness. I thought if I found a husband and had a family of my own that that would provide all the security and love I needed. I was deluded of course and subsequently found my life in a spiralling mess of pain and anguish.

As a teenager I started to feel pulled by the culture of clubbing, drink and boyfriends. Unfortunately I wasn't grounded enough in my faith at the point when the peer pressure became a real issue. I was somewhat impressionable. I started to look for love in relationships, going from one boyfriend to the next in a desperate attempt to find "the one".

With each relationship I became more damaged. My self worth was zapped as I compromised my morals and found myself partaking in all the things that I had thought I would never do. I put myself at risk emotionally and physically. By the time I was just twenty I had both a broken engagement and a miscarriage under my belt.

In 1998 I realised my goal of marriage. Unfortunately, however, my marriage lasted just six years and by age twenty-nine I was divorced.

Many people would probably say that their twenties were one of the best decades of their lives. Young, wrinkle free, and out of the sometimes "awkward" teenage stage, your whole life lays ahead of you with an abundance of opportunities. Sadly my twenties will not go down as the best years of my life, but they probably were the years during which I learnt the most lessons.

It was in my early twenties that I became ill. I started to develop quite severe abdominal pain and discomfort, which at its worse felt like severe cramping or "twisting" going on from the point of my belly button down to my bladder. I would also have sudden shooting pains that would instantly cause me to double up.

After about a year I became quite concerned. Doctors had put it down to Irritable Bowel Syndrome but none of the treatments for this were working and I felt the condition was worsening. I was suffering two weeks out of every four. At this time I was studying to become a Dispensing Optician. I was trying to juggle home life, a full time job and a Dispensing diploma all whilst feeling quite unwell.

I felt convinced it was something more than Irritable Bowel Syndrome and by keeping track of my symptoms I felt it was related to my monthly cycle and possibly a gynaecology problem. Eventually after seeing a different doctor I managed to get a referral to a Gynaecologist. After investigative surgery I was diagnosed with severe endometriosis. It had affected almost every organ in my lower abdomen.

Back to the Beginning

This diagnosis was a real blow to me. I had a real strong desire to be a mum and it was explained to me that my fertility might well have been affected. I was started on various forms of hormone treatment to try to reduce some of the lesions. All the treatments were gruelling and ongoing.

My body was often being put into a "pseudo" menopausal state in a hope that if my periods were staved off long enough some of the lesions would shrink and possibly disappear. I would get all the usual symptoms associated with the actual menopause including the debilitating hot flushes. It was explained to me, however, that it could potentially be the resulting "scar" tissue that would cause a threat to my fertility rather than the lesions themselves.

Treatments did help the pain aspect of the condition but I soon found that I had a very deep emotional pain associated with the thought of possible infertility. I felt like I had no way of dealing with that scenario. It was an unbearable thought for me not to be able to have children at some point in my life.

I longed to have children and just could not get my head around the possibility of it not happening. After a few years of treatment doctors were recommending that I try for children sooner than later but my marriage was failing and I was in no position to try for a baby. There was no way of knowing whether I was fertile or not.

By my mid twenties I found myself suffering with depression and anxiety. A combination of a rocky marriage, a full on work and study life and my endometriosis proved simply too much for me to cope with all at the same time. It didn't help in that my hormones were continually all over the place as a result of the medication I was on and this was, no doubt, not helping my emotions.

I reached a point where, although I would not have described myself as suicidal, if I had been offered a pill that would send me off in to a permanent sleep I'm quite sure I would have taken it without hesitation. I had never imagined that my life could be so painful. Every moment was an effort, I constantly felt drained and hopeless. My eyes were permanently swollen from crying. I had lost weight and looked terrible.

I would somehow manage my job and my course but at the end of each working day I would find myself downing a bottle of wine to myself for the simple fact that for just a few hours I would be out of it, out of the pain, out of the hopelessness.

As I reflected on my life and where the decisions I had made had landed me I found myself thinking about God again. It had been almost ten years since I had walked away from church and contrary to what I told others, I had never stopped believing.

I reflected back to my baptism when I was just 13. I have never forgotten the way I had felt at the time of my baptism and how tangible God's presence had been to me upon that special day. I recalled the scripture that had been read for me personally that amazing Baptism day. " I will never leave you nor forsake you" (Joshua 1: 5). That verse had been permanently etched into my memory and as I pondered over the words I started to feel that perhaps all was not lost. I began to wonder if there was a way back for me. Was there hope?

At work one day I met someone that was about to change my life completely. She was a customer of mine, a beautiful black young lady with an amazing smile I simply cannot explain. She had long plaited hair and a beautiful friendly face. Her character and her demeanour were somewhat different but I could not put my finger on how. We did not

Back to the Beginning 55

talk much other than for the purposes of dispensing her spectacles but for some reason she made a lasting impact on me. After this initial meeting at work I started to see this lady on various occasions, never to talk to, I would just look up and see her.

The first couple of times I didn't give it a second thought but after a while I started to think this was more than a coincidence. Firstly I realised that if I hadn't looked up at precise moments I would have missed her. There was one time I was in my car waiting my turn at a roundabout and I looked up to see her sat on a bus passing by. There were other times I saw her and it really was as though someone had lifted my head at the exact moment enabling me to see her before she was gone.

I finally realised what was happening when there was one instance where I had dropped my husband off at the train station very early in the morning. I had just pulled up outside my flat. I had put my head in my hands and the tears were uncontrollable. I had no idea how to continue; my strength was failing, and I was at my lowest ebb.

I then lifted my head and there she was, walking past my flat. Walking past my flat at 6.00 a.m.! What were the odds?! This time her eyes caught mine, she smiled and I simply looked at her stunned. This was to be the last time I would see her but her job was done. As I sat bemused in my car I realised that every time I had seen her, I had been at my lowest; at times when I had thought I simply could not continue.

Times when I was fighting the tears and feeling as though I was about to fall over the edge of the precipice I had been teetering on for so long. Seeing her had always helped me take just another step. She had helped me to persevere. There was little I knew of this individual other than one very important thing, her name. The one thing I had been reminded of each and every time I had seen her was her name ...... her name was Hope.

Whilst being prayed for once at my church, my pastor said that God had shown him that there had been times in my life when God had very literally saved me from disaster. As he spoke, scenes from my life flashed through my mind like a movie clip. I saw clearly how on many occasions God had intervened and changed the course of incidences in my life; ones that could have resulted in devastation. In one respect I felt shaken to the core, but on the other I was overcome with emotion as I realised the level of God's protection during the many years I had abandoned Him.

Throughout the entire time I was a prodigal, God was watching over me. Although I had walked away from God, He had never left me. Despite the damage as a result of my own wrong decisions in life, God had kept me from death, and loved me so much that He sent me an angel in human form to give me a message of hope that was to change my life forever.

Following this life changing event I began to seek God again. I started to pray for the first time in almost ten years. Each day, despite my circumstances, I found myself with an inner knowledge that my life would change. I felt sure there would be good times ahead of me. I even had an assurance that somehow I would, at some point in my life, become a mum. Whenever doubt crept in to my mind God would use something or someone to get another message of hope to me. I had letters arrive to me from family out of the blue.

They were written on notelets with the word hope on them. I had dreams and visions of a good and prosperous life. One very poignant moment for me was when I was coming around from an anaesthetic having had surgery to try to remove some of my endometriosis. There was a lady doctor waiting by my side. Seemingly aware of my inner concerns she gripped my hand. Her words flooded me with joy. "One of your ovaries looks fine so with regards to your fertility there is definitely hope". My future daughter was at that point named! Hope was everywhere.

8. Moving On

" God is my helper, the Lord is the sustainer of my soul" Psalm 54:4

At the start of each of our Sunday morning services we show a short DVD mainly for the benefit of visiting non-Christians. It starts off "We are all broken people, but Jesus is putting us back together". I was a broken person, harshly weathered from life's experiences but from the very moment I re-committed my life to God, a healing began in me as God began to very carefully pick up the broken shards of my life and put them back together again.

Following my marriage breakdown I lived with my parents for a while. Without hesitation I started to go with them to their church. I can best describe going back to church as "going home". The warmth of God's presence was welcoming, comforting and full of promise. I knew that the only way forward for me was God's way. So deeply hurt by walking my own path, I had sadly had to learn the hard way but as I re-committed my life to Christ my path was re-set. I was back on course and about to embark upon the most dramatic turnaround.

I quite often reflect on all the prayer that was going up for me during my "prodigal" years. I know particularly my parents and my late Nana interceded in prayer for me during that time. I am so grateful they did. If you have loved ones who have walked away from God I urge you to never stop praying for them. God will answer you.

During my time at Bible School we were taught to imagine our prayers for people and circumstances being put into "prayer bowls" in Heaven. The more you pray specifically for someone or something the deeper the bowl is filled. There will come a point when the bowl is full and when it is the bowl will tip releasing the fulfilment of the petitions over the situation. This can take time. In some cases we will not see the answers to our prayers in our life time even, but we need to trust that God does hear us, and will answer us.

My parents tell me that although it was difficult having to watch me make the mistakes I did that they did have an assurance it would turn out well at some point. They did not know when but they just kept trusting God to take care of me.

1 Thessalonians 5:17 says "Pray without ceasing". In other words, don't give up! I know especially for my Nana, she was so delighted to see the answers to her prayers for me in her lifetime.

When you pray for loved ones ask the Holy Spirit to be with them. Ask for the veil of deception to be lifted. Pray for divine appointments, for other Christians to come across their path. Pray for God to use circumstances in their lives to cause them to evaluate where they are. James 5: 16 says "The earnest, heartfelt, continued prayer of a righteous man makes tremendous power available".

As you pray God's power will be released into the situation. Sometimes, however, a situation has to reach an all time low before there is a breakthrough. That was what happened in my case. God gave us all free will and with my free will I chose to blot Jesus out of my life for a long time. It took my life crashing all about me to cause me to seek God again. But when I did finally seek him, he was there with open arms.

At the beginning of this new chapter of my life I had emotional scars that ran very deep. I had very little self worth. I despised my reflection and was constantly paranoid

Moving On

about how I looked, caking myself in make-up, unable to step outside the door without it.

I also had become quite painfully shy in new settings and venturing anywhere on my own was excruciating. I recall being asked to have a small part in the church Christmas play. I initially agreed but soon pulled out as the thought of being on "show" felt simply impossible.

I was generally an anxious person, finding reasons to worry in almost any situation. Despite all these issues I had every reason to be thankful. I was down but not out! I knew that as I devoted my life to God that the deep creases would be ironed out and I would emerge strong and confident.

I recently spoke at a singles conference held at our church. I had been asked to share on how I had moved on from divorce. My main advice to people was to do their best not to get into a POM state, a 'poor old me' state. I fell in to this initially and I believe it can be an almost natural response to hardship and low self-esteem.

I remember almost enjoying telling people of my years of hardship. I think I liked the reaction it got me and also the attention, and knowing people were feeling for me, in a strange way, made me feel special; something I had not felt in a long time. I did not recognise what I was doing at first but after a few months I realised I had moved in to a victim mentality and in doing so I was not only unhealthily dwelling on the past I was in danger of becoming reliant on others to build me up rather than letting God do the work in me.

There is obviously a very important place for counselling and sharing with others and I really benefited from some prayer counselling with my pastors, but the real healing started within me as I began to put my problems aside and to seek God earnestly.

As I spent more and more time praying, reading the word, listening to teaching resources and spending as much time at church as I could, I really felt an energising within me. I noticed a gradual reduction in my anxiety and a gradual increase in my self esteem. As I started to see God working in me this had the effect of urging me to press in deeper and so the healing continued.

I believe that as we seek God wholeheartedly and hand all our fears and hang ups completely over to God, we in effect, become pliable. We need to render ourselves pliable in God's hands so He can begin to mould and re-shape us in to the people we are called to be. He can't do this if we are trying to fix ourselves; if we are continually seeking reassurance from others rather than our Father.

God gave me a picture to help me understand how I needed to let Him do the work. In this picture I saw myself on an operating table. It appeared that I was having very serious surgery being carried out. The surgeon, however, had visibly shaky hands! God then showed me the surgeon more closely...the surgeon was me! In a fragile state I was trying to fix myself! I then witnessed God himself take over; His hands steady and secure and fully able to do whatever work was necessary.

Another key issue is forgiveness. In order for God to move in our lives, we need to have forgiven those who we feel have hurt us and we also need to forgive ourselves for the wrong decisions we have made. This can be hard, the latter especially, but as we allow God full access into our hearts, forgiveness does become possible and there is real release as a result. In handing everything to God we prevent bitterness from creeping into our lives.

When God comes in to our lives our hearts are softened and we begin to take on the nature of God. As I let God flow through me I literally felt my heart being transformed. There is no pain too big that God cannot heal, no situation

Moving On

too difficult for Him to completely turn around. God is able!

Very soon I was doing so much better. There were times of setbacks but, most importantly, I was headed in the right direction. My confidence was growing and I was starting to tell others about how God was changing my life. I moved into a beautiful, small but cosy, rented house and although still adjusting to single life, for the first time in years I was happy.

A really significant moment for me was when I gave my testimony at a small ladies Alpha group. A year prior to this it would have been impossible for me to say two words in front of a group and now I was telling my story! I was shaking like a leaf and moving my feet about continuously but never the less I was speaking in public! I could barely believe it!

From very early on in this journey I had really prayed that God would use what I had been through to help others. I was determined it would not all be in vain. As the years have gone on, the opportunities to encourage others have been countless. God can and will turn any situation around for good and use it for His glory if we allow him to.

9. My Soul Mate

"Record the vision, inscribe it on tablets, that the one who reads it may run. For the vision is yet for the appointed time, it hastens toward the goal and will not fail. Though it tarries, wait for it, for it will certainly come" Habakkuk 2:2- 3

As a Christian singleton I soon desired to be married again but this time to God's choice for me. I felt sure this was part of God's plan for me but I had no idea at what point in my life this would happen. I would spend a lot of time thinking of what my future husband would be like; what he would do for a living and how we would meet.

I believe as long as you remain careful not to let a desire all consume you, there is no harm in spending time visualising things. In fact I believe God wants us to use our God given imaginations to positively picture our desires and ambitions. In spending time imagining a good marriage and a good future I was acting in faith.

Something I heard preached one day about the importance in "writing the vision" prompted me to do, what I believe, was a very significant task. I decided I would write a list of all the qualities and attributes I wanted in my future spouse. There were, in total, 15 points in my list, ranging from the importance of a steadfast faith to the importance of them being able to make me laugh.

One of my most important requisites was that my husband to be would want a family with me. This to me was imperative. Constantly recalling my angel of hope gave me this huge assurance that I would be a mum. I so wanted to be a mum and as my 30th birthday loomed I started to feel my biological clock ticking!

In August 2004, on a beautiful hot day, I travelled to Shoreham near Brighton. A friend had invited me to spend the day on his Scuna boat with some of his other friends as he changed the boat's mooring from Shoreham to Eastbourne harbour. It was on this boat that I initially met Graham. Graham was a friend of this person too.

He was a member of the Eastbourne group of our church movement. There was warmth to Graham that instantly endeared me to him. I thought he was extremely handsome. He was about 5 inches smaller than me however! My first impression was that he was aged around 38 but I thought perhaps he could be a little older as he had one of his teenage sons with him.

His dark hair was shaven short, which I liked. I felt an instant connection with him and as we began to talk and the boat sailed deep in to the ocean, hard as it may be to believe, I'm quite sure I started to fall in love with him.

Graham too was a divorcee, recent as in my case. We had both been broken people within whom God was doing a tremendous work. The boat we were sailing on that day was named Soteria. We did not realise it at the time but we learnt last year that the meaning of Soteria is restoration, healing and salvation!

Our meeting that day was no co-incidence, it was a God ordained meeting, the very name of the boat mirroring exactly what God was to do in both our lives as he would later knit us together in the union of marriage, giving us both a second chance at love.

Graham was simply lovely. I loved everything about him. He had two sons, the eldest Daniel, then 17 and Matthew 15, both living with him at the time. I saw in him a passion for God, a passion for the lost and a passion to see lives changed. As we parted at the end of the day I watched Graham walk off along the jetty in front of me. We had not exchanged numbers but something in me simply knew that our paths would cross again.

Before I had met Graham I had already toyed with the idea of moving to a new town, potentially Eastbourne. I had decided that this would be a good thing to do; a fresh start away from the town that, despite the healing taking place within me, held many a difficult memory.

I had thought about a move to Eastbourne, just 30 minutes down the coast. Eastbourne is the most amazing seaside resort. They call it the Sunshine Coast, and it is just that. Its promenade resembles what I would expect to find somewhere in the Mediterranean with beachside coffee houses and quaint eateries.

The summers here are renowned to be hot and sunny. It is a beautiful, well kept, up and coming town. It appealed to me even more now I had met Graham! The firm I worked for had a branch there and so I broached my work about a possible transfer. I was delighted to be told that this would be possible and so I had started to look in to housing in the area.

In January 2005 I made a visit to Eastbourne Christian Outreach Centre as I knew having a good church home would be imperative for me. I clearly remember the drive over there. My dad was kindly escorting me for a bit of moral support. I remember wondering whether I would see Graham and how would I feel about that. How would he respond to me?

Would it be awkward? Was I trying to force our paths to cross again rather than leaving it to God? I was a blur of thoughts and emotions but with or without Graham being in the picture I felt sure I wanted to move somewhere new and wanted to see how I found the Eastbourne church in comparison to my church home in Hastings, which I absolutely loved.

I did see Graham again and yes it was awkward! He looked shocked to see me. I was so pleased to see him again and not at all surprised by the warm feelings I still felt towards him, which were the same as when I met him that beautiful day the previous year on Soteria.

Graham asked my dad and I back to his house for dinner but we had arranged to see my Nan so I had to decline. After briefly chatting at the end of the service we said our goodbyes, again! I felt frustrated in that I knew how I felt about him, but I didn't think that was coming across!

Graham had asked me out when we met on the boat, but in shock I had quite bluntly said "it wasn't the right time", and then had failed to come up with any positive after remark that would have given him any hope!

Now I had just turned an offer down again! The following month I visited the church again, and received another dinner offer that I had to decline! We still had not exchanged numbers! On my third visit to the church I handed Graham an invite to my 30th birthday fancy dress party. He finally had my number!

As I handed him the invitation I remember thinking "I do hope he gets the message now!" I prayed he would come, but in honesty at this point I was not sure he would. There would be hardly anyone he knew there and he didn't really know me! Giving Graham the invite was my way of saying, "Graham I really like you, I want to see you again, please come," but with all the times I had declined his dinner offers I wondered whether he would feel totally confused. I was obviously giving off mixed feelings even though this was totally not my intention!

Days before my party, I had had no response from Graham as to whether he was coming or not. I tried not to think of how disappointed I would be if he didn't come. On the evening of my party I was dressed as a blue fairy. I wore this beautiful blue fairy dress with wings and a tiara in my hair. I was also covered in glitter! I was a strange sight as on my left foot I wore a pretty white sandal and then on my right foot I wore a chunky plaster cast following an operation I had undergone recently. The 30 year old blue fairy with the huge plaster casted foot on a pair of crutches hurriedly limped to the door every time the bell went, desperately hoping to see Graham on the doorstep!

As the evening went on there was no sign of Graham, just lots of strangely dressed friends who had done their best to join in the silliness of the occasion for my benefit! Then, finally he arrived! The moment I opened the door to see him standing there my heart leapt with joy, although of course I tried to remain seemingly cool!

I remember thinking how handsome he was, dressed simply in a shirt and jeans. He had not come dressed in fancy dress but I wasn't at all worried about that. It was blatantly obvious to all that evening how smitten I was with him! It was like being a teenager all over again!

I followed him everywhere. I liked the way he simply fitted in! He was outgoing and confident. My feelings were growing! At the end of the evening Graham announced he was going. I felt sure he would ask me out so I offered to walk him to his car to give him the opportunity. As he opened the door to get in it suddenly dawned on me that he wasn't going to ask me!

Why? Surely he had got the message that evening! I had followed him around all night! There was no way I was going to let him drive away without telling him how I felt. So I just blurted it out! "Graham I know I have turned you down several times before but would you like to go out to dinner sometime?" I stood, nervously awaiting his response.

"Yeah probably!" he replied and promptly got in his car and took off! The blue fairy was left standing on her driveway, knocked off her perch! I stood there in shock for a few moments before meandering back to my guests. I was, for want of a nicer phrase, gutted! Absolutely gutted! "Probably", what kind of an ambiguous response was that, I thought.

As I said goodbye to the remainder of my guests I tried to hide my disappointment, then "beep beep, beep, beep" my phone sounded. I opened the text. It was Graham. "Did I say probably, what I meant was "DEFINITELY!" I smiled. The rest, as they say, is history!

Graham and I were married six months later. It was a beautiful but modest occasion and it was just perfect. It was a very special day to mark the start of a very special future together as Mr and Mrs Compton.

10. The Shared Desire

" Hope in God for I will yet praise you, the Hope of my countenance" Psalm 42:5

Newly married life was even better than I imagined it would be. There was so much laughter in my life; so much joy. God's love through Graham has been a huge part of my restoration. It is so clear to me that Graham and I were meant to be. Meeting on the boat Soteria, was just one of the many confirmations we have had.

Within just a few months of our marriage I could see great improvements in my confidence and self esteem. I knew Graham loved me and I knew he saw me as beautiful inside and out. Graham was the first man with whom I could truly relax and be myself.

It was totally liberating for me to not be worrying whether I was looking my best all the time. I could relax and it was great. For the first time I began to be happy with the reflection in the mirror and for the first time I could look at my whole face in one go, without squinting to blur the view I previously hated with a passion.

Graham knew all about my past, as I did his. When I met Graham I was still very fragile, in the very early stages of my recovery. Things were still quite raw. I was very insecure and negative and still not firmly grounded in my faith. I was certainly an individual with whom Graham needed clarity from God about.

But God gave Graham all the assurance he needed. God revealed to him the potential within me and He showed him the real Mel; the Mel that would be following a period of healing. Graham tells me that it was like God gave him a glimpse of how I would develop as I continued in my walk with Him.

From the very beginning of our marriage Graham and I knew that we wanted to pursue the possibilities of having children together. This, unlike in my first marriage, was a desire we both shared. However, there were two major factors that, on the face of it, appeared to be big obstacles in the way of this desire becoming reality.

Firstly there was my endometriosis. All the treatment I had had over the years had kept the illness at bay and at a manageable level, but it was still there and in fact in the early part of our marriage it was proving to be quite a recurrent problem for me and the pain at times was quite severe.

The other obstacle was that Graham had had a vasectomy about thirteen years before I met him. He was in essence, infertile! The situation seemed almost impossible. I recall the time when Graham first mentioned his vasectomy; it had been during a telephone conversation in the early stages of our dating.

By this time I already felt certain he was the one, and had been imagining our future together. I had allowed myself to become excited about the prospect of having the children I had yearned to have for so long. When he told me, I felt my heart literally sink; I was speechless and instantly drained. How? Why? What?! This was last thing I had wanted to hear!

Why would God, knowing my desires, give me an infertile husband? What about the promise of a daughter, Hope? There were days of confusion and anguish for me following this revelation from Graham. But ultimately it was a no brainer and there was no way my decision to marry Graham could or would be affected by this news. My fertility was in question too and how would I feel if this thwarted Graham's decision to be with me!

The Shared Desire

When Graham and I entered marriage, we entered it with a steadfast hope that God could do a miracle for us although we did not know how or when. We held fast to the promise I knew God had given me ... the promise of a baby daughter, Hope.

With Graham being 42 and me 30 we decided that we would not wait to pursue our dream of children together. We talked, and prayed about how best to go about it. There was a couple in our church who became aware of our circumstance. Like us, the husband was older than his wife.

He had had children to a previous partner and had subsequently had a vasectomy. They desperately wanted a family together and sought God for a miracle. This couple came to dinner with us one Sunday afternoon and they shared their story.

They had had a vasectomy reversal carried out and had been given less than 20% chance of it being a success. Within just weeks of the operation they were pregnant. They had a beautiful little girl and they went on to have another girl just a short while later. It was a miracle.

They shared with us how they never even considered they would not be able to have children together. It was a strong desire they both shared and they knew God would somehow make it happen for them. To them having the vasectomy reversal was an act of faith. Ignoring the statistical odds of it being a success they went ahead regardless.

After giving it much thought and prayer Graham and I decided that this was the route we would take; we would try for a vasectomy reversal. This was not something available on the NHS so we needed to go privately. Like our friends, we were given quite low odds for it being a success. It was explained to us that the longer the period from when the original vasectomy had been done, the less likely the reversal would be effective.

The plumbing, if you like, could be re-connected but the body can have a tendency to build up resilience to the sperm over the years and actually cause the sperm to become immotile and therefore inactive. There was also the consideration of my endometriosis.

Graham could go through the distress of a painful operation only to find that I was unable to conceive anyway. We decided we would go for this procedure anyway. Just a few months after we were married Graham underwent rather painful surgery to attempt to reverse his vasectomy. As I nursed him at home following this operation I was moved by what he had been prepared to go through for me, for us and for our desires. He was, to say the least, tender!

The months following the reversal were somewhat nail-biting for me. Early tests revealed that sperm was now coming through but there was very little and a lot of it was completely dead, as had been feared by the professionals.

We were, however, encouraged to keep trying. Sadly with each routine sperm test following the operation the levels of viable sperm decreased until the point where the tests were showing nothing but immotile sperm.

When the news came through about the last and final test results we were both knocked sideways for some time. For about a week we were both quite lifeless, but God was teaching us both to trust; to completely lean on him and not our own understanding of the situation as it appeared. After a while we emerged fresh with hope and anticipation again. We had hit a hurdle but we would keep going and refuse to quit!

After a few months we went back to the fertility clinic for some further advice. Despite Graham's sperm being immotile there was one form of fertility treatment that we were told might be effective in our case. It was called ICSI (Intracytoplasmic Sperm Injection). This treatment is basically almost identical to IVF except for one stage. With both IVF and ICSI the woman's ovaries are stimulated using high levels of hormones over a period of time to produce multiple eggs. These eggs are then obtained by surgery and then, using sperm, they attempt to fertilise the harvested eggs. In IVF, motile sperm are placed with the eggs and any resulting conception is, "natural" if you like, despite taking place outside the body and in the laboratory. In our case obviously IVF was ruled out, due to the immobility aspect of Graham's sperm. With ICSI, the immotile sperm, unable by themselves to penetrate the eggs are, in fact, injected in to the eggs directly.

To embark with ICSI was a huge decision to make. Any form of such fertility treatment is very testing on the woman particularly. The percentage success rate was low, around 25% chance of conception over three cycles of attempted treatment. We were advised that the first cycle would probably not be successful and of course the cost of the treatment would increase with every cycle of treatment necessary.

With much to think and pray about we decided to give it some time before embarking on any further treatment. We knew that God could in fact do a miracle without any further treatment. We also knew that he could also work through the treatment. In the summer of 2006 we planned that in 6 months time, January 2007, we would embark with ICSI treatment, unless we had fallen pregnant naturally, of course, or if God had closed the door on the treatment for some reason. You often hear faith being described as "action".

With a plan of action now in place Graham and I felt really positive. We knew to be in faith was to move in faith and that was what we considered we were doing.

It had become apparent to us, that within Christian circles particularly, the ethics of IVF and particularly ICSI were under debate. We fully respected the opinions of others, but from our perspective we could not see anything ethically wrong with IVF or ICSI providing it was my eggs and Graham's sperm being used. The issue of the freezing of eggs and unused embryos for future use concerned us but there was the option to refuse that action available.

To us, ICSI was an avenue through which God could move, and we trusted Him that if it wasn't the right route for us that he would give us clarity of mind accordingly.

Over the coming months we sought God earnestly. If ICSI was not right and it was, in fact, desperation pushing us in that direction, we wanted God to show us clearly. We also sought counsel from loved ones and our pastors. We had a great network of faith-filled and positive people around us to help us through.

Around this time a very significant and wonderful thing happened to me... I was healed of my endometriosis! I had been prayed for many a time for this condition but as yet had not experienced my breakthrough. I knew this issue was key to my conceiving and carrying children. We had a guest speaker at our church one weekend and he had a word of knowledge for someone with multiple lesions that God wanted to heal.

This fitted my condition exactly as that was precisely how my endometriosis presented itself: many womb tissue lesions adhered to many organs in my abdomen including my bladder and ovaries. I responded to this word of knowledge and went forward for prayer.

There was no surge of heat or tingling, I simply felt a peace flood over me and I had an inner confidence and firm belief this condition was about to become history! After the time of ministry had finished our Pastor asked from the front "Does anyone feel they have received a healing today?" Without me even thinking about it, my arm shot right up. This time of prayer had felt different. It was my time and I truly believed my endometriosis would now be a thing of the past. As I write this, over three years on, I have not so much as had a twinge in my abdomen since! Praise God. The timing of my miracle was perfect.

The months leading up to our treatment came with both anticipation and excitement and also some disappointment at times. Each month I obviously hoped I would conceive naturally, especially now the obstacle of my endometriosis was no longer.

I remember one month my period was exceptionally late. Coincidently I was also feeling rather sick and exhausted. I was on the bus to work one morning and I came over particularly faint. The bus was hot and jam-packed and I began to feel the edges of my vision go. "Not on the bus!" I called out to God in my head. "Please don't let me faint now!".

Fortunately I gradually came too without fully collapsing amidst all the people. After recovering from the incident, and now off the busy bus, I became very excited, feeling absolutely sure I was pregnant. I was at work all day itching to announce to someone I was pregnant and I was desperate to buy a test and wee on it!

The following day, first thing in the morning I took a test...Negative. That day was one of the most difficult days during that season of my life. I found myself bent over in physical anguish. I curled myself up in a ball at the foot of my bed and cried out to God. The journey seemed too hard at this point.

The path to motherhood for most women is relatively straight forward yet for others like myself it is an emotional rollercoaster of highs and lows, positive days and days of sheer agony. There were days when I simply could not seem to shake off the doubt and the fears. Yet on other days I was full of positive anticipation. I constantly had to force myself to remember all the promises God had given me.

There were times when it seemed it was all I could think about, and then I'd feel rotten that I had let it consume me so much. That particular day, the day of the negative test, we had invited our neighbour and her children to a barbeque at our home. She had a two-year-old little boy and twin boys, just a few months old. Every inch of me wanted to cancel. How could I possibly face having newly born babies at my home, not just one, but two! With God's help I managed it graciously; my face was getting used to the brave look by this stage!

After my experiences I have so much empathy for women who struggle to conceive or carry babies. There are barely words to describe the pain and anguish connected to such an issue. To be a woman; to have periods; to have a womb and ovaries and yet struggle to conceive or carry babies to term I believe is one of the most heart wrenching difficulties we can encounter in life.

There is such frustration and pain associated with it, and on that particular day I was feeling that very pain. Without God in my life I feel quite sure my emotions would not have survived such an ordeal. That evening I found myself again at the foot of my bed. By my bedside was a Christian magazine I had not yet had a chance to look through.

Picking it up and randomly opening it I came across an article that would serve to renew my hope, stir my faith again and give me strength to continue. It was the testimony of a woman; a pastor of a large well known and respected church in this country. She told her story of how a few years in to her marriage she had found out she had severe fertility problems. She describes her and her husband's journey as

The Shared Desire 79

they embarked on a gruelling course of fertility treatment in their quest to have a child they so longed for.

She documented the emotional ups and downs as they went through eight cycles of treatment without any success. She talked of how God was the "anchor of her soul" during this time and how she absolutely refused to give up on this God given desire. Finally after several years they gave birth to a daughter and her name was...yes you have guessed it...HOPE!!!!!

Through every part of this season of my life God never failed to remind me of His personal promise to me. Whenever Satan began to get his foot in the doorway, God slammed it shut with his promises! Those lifelines just kept coming! Doubt and discouragement will threaten to swallow up the majority of Christians during times of difficulty.

This does not make us failures. It just makes us human! Sometimes a situation can seem so dire in the natural that you feel so far down the pit you can't see any light at all. When you are in a pit what you need is hope. Hope is well described as "a picture of a preferred future, a good resolve and good outcome".

One of the things I did to renew my hope was to draw a picture. I love art, so drawing comes quite naturally for me. I drew a picture of myself walking hand in hand with two children: a boy and a girl. At this point I obviously had no idea that I would go on to have a boy and a girl. I felt certain God had promised me Hope but for some reason I found myself drawing a picture of a little boy too. In my picture, which I drew from the back view, I was holding the hand of a little girl on my left and a slightly taller boy on my right. I was obviously drawing a picture of my "preferred future"; what I felt was the ideal: two children, one of each.

My drawing revealed the desires of my heart; desires that are God-given. Reflecting back, I believe this picture to have been very significant. I now have an "actual" photo that mimics my drawing of 5 years ago exactly!

God wants us to have hope in every situation. This is why it is so beneficial to spend time picturing your "preferred future". If you are longing for a child, picture them and picture what they might look like. Imagine your first Christmas together; their first steps and words. If it is a husband or wife you are praying for, imagine them, picture your wedding day!

Know that God is for you and that His plans are good. If you have loved ones that do not know Jesus picture them saved, in church worshipping with you. As it is written in the book of Habakuk, "write the vision". As you do your hope will be stirred and it will become your anchor. Hope is the "energy" needed to reach your desired destination. As we entrust our lives and the lives of our loved ones to God, He becomes our source of hope.

Even if you or your loved ones are where you are because of your own doing, God can set you back in line for your destiny. Make a firm decision to fight off negative thoughts and strive to think positively, even if every inch of you seems to be pulling in the opposite direction.

Romans 5:5 says "Hope does not disappoint because the love of God has been poured out within our hearts". Hope will keep you going; energise you; get you out of your bed and steer you towards the light.

11. A New Year

"Never doubt in the darkness what God told you in the light" Dr Bob Jones Sr

In January 2007 Graham and I began I.C.S.I. treatment. We had total peace about our decision. We knew we had God's complete backing following months of prayer and counsel. We felt sure this was putting our faith into action. God had not closed the door for us.

We had been accepted and we had sufficient funds available for a 'three attempt' course of treatment. As we drove up to the hospital for our first appointment we both felt excited about the potential outcome of what we were about to embark on.

I had to very rapidly overcome my fear of needles as, on our first appointment, I was shown how to inject the daily hormone myself directly into my stomach. Either I master it myself or I would have to visit the hospital each day to have a nurse do it for me. I was somewhat offended by the nurse's comment about how, if I put the needle into the flabby part of my belly, it would be less painful!

But what she said was true, and for the first time ever I was grateful that I had a bit of padding there! The daily injections never became exactly easy for me. I would become quite flustered each time before plunging the needle in. It never failed to make me cringe but I always managed it and was always highly proud once I had done it.

Despite the amount of hormones I was pumping inside me I was fortunate in that, at that stage, I did not have any emotional side effects from them. In fact, apart from the trauma of the daily injections, I felt quite well. I could feel my ovaries working though, but it was not painful, just a little uncomfortable. The aim of the injections was to get my ovaries to produce multiple eggs. For some women this does not happen as it should; for others the ovaries can be over stimulated to a dangerous level. If this were to happen then the treatment would be stopped immediately.

I tried not to think of the natural odds of it working. The consultant had reiterated over and over about the treatment not being expected to work first time. They viewed it merely as a trial run, to see how my body responded to the hormones; to establish what changes to make for the second attempt.

I was so very aware of God's peace throughout the whole time and with each day that passed we became more confident and certain that we were about to realise our dream.

After about 4 weeks of injections a scan revealed that the hormones had successfully stimulated my ovaries and my eggs were ready for collection. I was booked in for day surgery. That same day Graham's sperm would be collected and they would attempt fertilisation. Three days on from that, providing any conception had taken place, up to two fertilised eggs would be surgically implanted in my womb.

The day of the egg collection will go down to be one of the most memorable and surreal days of our lives. Up to that point regular checks on Graham's sperm had revealed there was enough immotile yet viable sperm that could be used for the treatment.

However, on the critical day there was none! I will never forget the moment the doctor came and stood at the foot of my bed. I was coming around from the anaesthetic having just had a successful egg collection. Graham was by my bedside. The doctor seemed physically pained to tell us that there was absolutely no viable sperm in Graham's sample. We were totally stunned. I felt the life drain out of me as the ramifications of such an announcement hit me. No viable sperm; no fertilisation. All we had been through to date, completely useless. Graham was asked to do another sample. The wait for the results of this second sample seemed a lifetime.

Graham and I could barely talk, no doubt processing everything in our own ways. It was like I could see my dream drifting away and I felt powerless to do anything about it. In that moment I felt as though God had just left. I did not feel his peace or his presence.

It was like I was grieving, a deep void just opened up instantly. What I was obviously experiencing was shock. Surely God was not closing the door at this stage? Had we missed his guidance with regards to this treatment? Had we gone the wrong way? All these thoughts ran through my mind. At that moment I was totally convinced this was the end of the road. If there no longer was any viable sperm, no further cycles of treatment would be possible. That would be that.

Graham sat at my side; although silent like me he was dealing with the matter very differently. When I was weak, he kept strong and I am so thankful he did. Graham's faith was being stirred not thwarted by this seemingly impossible situation. He was refusing to give up and he began to call out to God with all he had.

Now alone in our private room, he got out of his chair and began pacing the floor. For Graham this was the chance to see our God move, our God step in and make a way where there seemed no way. I could almost see the defiance swell in his expression as he refused to allow all to be lost.

He began to quote Psalm 91, over and over. I, on the other hand, remained lifeless. I was pleased to see Graham's determination but I was quite convinced it was all in vain. My heart sunk as the doctor came back in the room. I felt certain there would be more bad news. I braced myself. I wanted to block my ears as I could not figure how I would deal with such a blow. Then, "We have some viable sperm," the doctor announced! "Not much but we at least have a chance" he added. "Whoosh", I felt the hope flush back into my veins.

The doctor then went on to say how he had contacted the surgeon who had carried out Graham's initial vasectomy reversal. The doctors had been thinking how they could maximise the chances of my eggs being fertilised.

Although this second sample had been better they explained to us there was still very little viable sperm they could use and that the odds of any of it being strong enough for fertilisation were very low. However, they explained if they operated on Graham and took the sperm from source then they may have a better chance. The surgeon was free and willing to come to the hospital immediately to operate if Graham was happy.

Slowly taking in all we were being told, it was nothing short of surreal! What were the odds of this turn around? Firstly, why were they all so keen to go out of their way beyond the normal extents of their duties? Secondly, what were the odds of the top, highly sought after surgeon being available and willing to drop what he was doing and come in to carry out surgery there and then?!

We had waited months to get an appointment with him before and now he was willing to carry out unscheduled surgery at a moment's notice! To top it all off, one of the fertility nurses, was happy to work late, beyond the end of their long shift to work on the fertilisation!

The entire situation had been completely turned around in an instant. It had God written ALL over it!! Before we had a chance to digest all that was happening I was out of bed and Graham was in bed and being prepped for his surgery!

The day was getting on by this stage and it was now early evening and there was a change of nursing staff. Excited and re-enthused about our situation we were brimming with happiness! The nurse that came on to her night shift and came to check on Graham was obviously instantly aware of our hopeful anticipation.

In the short time we had we were able to witness to her. We shared how we were Christians and how we believed God had just completely turned our situation around for his glory. She was completely open to all we had to share. I had sometimes wondered why it was taking all this treatment in a fertility clinic for me to conceive.

Why could I not have just got pregnant without all of this? Now as I listened to Graham share the gospel with the nurse we would not have met if not for the bizarre turn of events, I thought how if this was all for the ultimate salvation of one individual such as this nurse, then that alone made it all completely worthwhile.

Three days following this surreal day I had two embryos implanted in to my womb and just two embryos had successfully fully fertilised; the exact number as was legally allowed to be implanted in a woman of my age, thus making any potential dilemma regarding remaining viable embryos a non-issue for us.

The attending nurse at the procedure, aware of the bizarre events of three days previously, looked at me and said, "two perfect embryos, it does not get any better than that".
Those words were like honey to my soul. Graham and I had

the privilege of seeing the embryos under a microscope before they were implanted.

They appeared exactly like a child would draw a flower head with a circle in the middle and further circles around the outside. It was a hugely moving experience to see them right at the beginning of their journey. I knew without a shadow of a doubt from that day that God had given us two children, Hope and Isaac …. complete miracles.

Exactly two weeks following implantation was test day. At 5.00 a.m. in the morning Graham and I awoke and sat up in bed at exactly the same time, and I mean at precisely the same moment! Another bizarre yet by this stage half-expected phenomenon during this experience! The line on the pregnancy test was clear and strong. Huddled together on the bathroom floor we hugged and wept tears of joy as we praised God for all his goodness to us and for his amazing miracle working power.

After many tears of joy, Graham and I went back to bed for more rest. I turned, lay on my side and looked at my bedside table. On it sat two pairs of tiny booties, one pink, and one blue, bought for me by Graham the year before. A bold and steadfast act of Graham's faith was now to be rewarded with little precious feet to fit.

My advice to anyone considering fertility treatment especially IVF and ICSI is to, first and foremost, take a good amount of time to think and pray about it. It is certainly not something to be embarked upon lightly. What may be right for one couple may not be for another. Make sure as a couple you are completely in agreement about it first and that your relationship together is in a healthy place.

It is emotional for the man as well as the woman and you need to be able to support each other through the entire process. Make sure you have a good network of trusted friends or family to support you through this time, especially in prayer.

I had about three trusted friends who I could really open up to about how I was feeling along my ISCI journey and this was invaluable to me. Be prepared, as you are likely to have well-meaning people share their conflicting views on the issue, and this can throw you if you are not careful. At the end of the day, it is your decision and I firmly believe that if you are walking closely to God that he will direct you along the path that is best for you.

I am saddened when I hear stories of women who wait years to have a baby without ever seeking medical assistance. They may well be holding on to a promise or a word spoken over them many years previously. Whilst I wholeheartedly admire their faith and steadfastness I wonder if some women miss their opportunity when some form of professional help may have proved a success.

Sometimes a very basic form of fertility treatment is all that is required; a lot of which is available under the NHS. I believe that God can and does work alongside the expertise of professionals in this area. Graham and I had our treatment at a private hospital near our home. The whole fertility unit had such a warm feel to it.

I expected the whole process to feel cold and clinical but for me it wasn't that way at all. I feel quite sure some of the staff were Christians themselves, and everyone we encountered was so clearly wanting to do all they could to help us maximise the chances of us realising our dream. Whenever my husband and I drive past the hospital we can't help but smile. I will never forget being in the waiting room for our very first appointment there.

On the table was a fertility magazine. One of the first things I read talked of how most people who really desire children could go on to have them whether naturally, with assistance or via fostering or adoption. It could, however, be a difficult road.

This was not a Christian magazine but I remember thinking how much hope that small passage could be giving to the people who read it. It was basically saying, if you chose not to give up there is likely to be a way somehow. It may not be the way you had planned it however. I thought how encouraging that was and how, with God on our side too, our determination could surely be rewarded.

As I write this chapter Hope and Isaac are almost three years of age, yet I remember their conception as if it were yesterday. Despite their prematurity they are now healthy and developing well. They are truly amazing. Hope is dark haired and green eyed with porcelain skin. Her head is now perfectly shaped and in our opinion, she is obviously the most beautiful little girl ever!

She loves dancing and singing and jumping around like Tigger! She is a very brave little girl who never makes a fuss when she is ill. Nothing much seems to faze her and the larger the climbing frame the better! To look at she is my absolute double. My parents say it is just like seeing me as a little girl all over again which I know is something really special for them.

About 4 years ago I was at the opening ceremony of a Christian conference and I found myself totally absorbed by a beautiful worship dance. As I watched the girls worship God in this way I was drawn to this one young girl. I would imagine she was in her mid teens. She was beautiful and elegant, with dark hair and porcelain skin. She was obviously gifted in dance and quite clearly loved Jesus. As I watched, I heard a soft voice in my heart, "That's Hope". "She will have that elegance; she will have that gifting".

I sometimes wondered whether that was my voice, or had God really spoken to me? As I look at Hope now there is no longer any doubt in my mind. Daily I watch Hope worship Jesus to her praise music. Her most favourite thing in life is dancing and as she dances and sings to Jesus she lifts up her little hands. She is elegant and beautiful just like the girl I watched four years ago.

Our precious Isaac is blonde and blue eyed. We call him our "big little man" as he towers over most toddlers his age and it is so hard to imagine how small he once was! Like Hope, he is hugely energetic! Isaac is a great people person, and loves interacting with people of all ages. He is very affectionate. Not long ago he insisted on holding my hand the entire time he was eating his cereal.

It was one of those moments you know you will never forget. Like most little boys he is car and train mad, "car" and "choo-choo" being some of his very first words, before "mummy", I might add!

Hope and Isaac are such a huge blessing, not only to us but to all who know them. For everyone that knows their story they are a permanent reminder of Gods' miracle working power, grace and love.

Raising twins is, however, no walk in the park! Emotionally, physically and logistically having two bundles of bursting energy the same age can be a daily mission and requires much patience, organisation and energy! It is non-stop from dawn till dusk and can be absolutely exhausting.

I remember being at one of my anti natal classes and the midwife was getting us to draw a pie chart of what activities our days would need to include having a new born baby. "Put in eight, fifteen minute sessions of feeding times," she said. Then, remembering one person in her class was an expectant mother of twins, she looked over at me "and yes for you Melanie you need to put in sixteen!".

I breast fed for about a month but then my milk decided to completely disappear for some unknown reason. I was actually quite relieved to be honest because this meant that Graham could help share the load. Graham got up with me for every night feed and I don't recall him moaning once!

Graham and I were with Hope and Isaac shopping in our local supermarket one day when we saw a very young couple, probably still in their teens, pushing triplets in what can only be described as the "Hummer Limo" of all push chairs! I have never seen anything like it; the push chair was huge! I have not seen this couple again but I often think of them and how they are coping. I wonder if they look quite so young and fresh faced now?

I have figured out that everything difficult regarding raising little ones comes in stages - stages that come and go before long. So although things like night feeds, teething, and tantrums can all be challenging, it's never that long before that season comes to an end. No matter how tired I get in my busy role of full time mummy I try my best not to moan. Whenever I feel a grumble coming I'm quick to remind myself of what a huge blessing Hope and Isaac are and what an honour it is to be entrusted with their care and spiritual growth.

Life post birth has come with a few health difficulties for me, especially as my hormone levels took quite a time to re-adjust. I had hoped to escape post natal depression but after about four months and some initial denial I had to face up to the fact I was being affected by it. The anxiety also started to become an issue again - not to the same degree and not in the same form as before - but needless to say it was there for a time.

I recall thinking how such a blessing could be accompanied by so much difficulty, but then I realised there had not been a day go by when God had not provided me with the necessary strength and grace to do all I had needed to do. Not only that, but I realised there had not been a day go by when at some point I had not laughed, smiled or felt carried along by a sense of hope. People often ask me, "How on earth do you cope with pre- school twins?" I reply, "With the help of the two G's, God and Graham!". Not forgetting a great family and friend support network.

12. The Strongest, Most Beautiful Butterfly

" Do not call to mind the former things or ponder things of the past, behold I will do something new, it will spring forth, will you not be aware of it. I will even make a roadway in the wilderness" Isaiah 43:18

"The strongest most beautiful butterflies are the ones that persevere the most." These were the words on a card a close friend gave to me on the very evening my waters broke. This same friend once said to me, "Sometimes, stuff just happens." I found that such a profound statement.

Looking back on the "stuff" that has happened to me over the last few years I recognise that some was because of my own life choices and some, well, just "because". I had often been quick to attribute situations to the enemy but I now realise that in doing so I was, in fact, giving satan the credit for things that were not in his power to do!

We need to remember daily that satan is DEFEATED! I recall the lyrics from a song regarding the enemy: "He makes mountains out of molehills"! Similar to the bruise analogy, satan can make things seem worse than they actually are.

He attempts to attack the mind, trying to generate a feeling of hopelessness, but we need to remember that we are far from hopeless when we walk with God! Our lives are full of hope! There is nothing that happens to us that God does not know about in advance. He knows what we can cope with and what we cannot. He understands every area of our strengths and weaknesses. He is constantly working within us to perfect all that concerns us and he carries our cares, our desires and our dreams at the forefront of his mind continuously.

Being a Christian does not exempt us from difficulties. It does, however, always provide us with the strongest pillar of strength to lean on. Corrie Ten Boom said "Never be afraid to trust an unknown future to a known God." I was studying Psalm 23 recently and I came across the passage that reads: "your rod and staff they comfort me".

Trying to conclude in my mind what this meant, I asked my mentor, Graham. He explained how in biblical times most men would have carried a staff. Upon their staff they would etch "memory triggers" of how God had answered their prayers over the years regarding different issues and circumstances in their lives.

Similar to how some of us may "journal". When you feel uncertain in a situation it is good to remember how God has come through for you before and how he will continue to come through for you throughout your life.

There came a point in my Christian walk when I thought " I either need to believe the word of God or not. I can't just believe bits of it: it's all or nothing." I remember my Dad saying the exact same thing to me once. When we read that God is our refuge and strength we have to believe it. When we read that we will not be shaken we must believe it.

When we read we are righteous we must know it and so on and so forth. One of my most favourite verses is " Hope in God for I shall yet praise him, the help of my countenance and my God". Between Psalm 42 and 43 alone we see it printed three times! And likewise we often see other verses repeated several times throughout the Bible.

The Strongest, Most Beautiful Butterfly   95

When we want someone to really grasp something we often repeat ourselves until we are sure the person has understood us. Similarly I see how God wants us to really get hold of his promises to us, and knowing our human tendency to doubt, He repeats things in an attempt to get His word embedded within us.

I once heard a very simple yet impacting message based around Romans 8: 28 "All things work together for good for those who love God." Basically, if we can come to that place where we know the word of God to be true, we can come to that place where we can be free of all fear for we just know that we know that all things (not just some!) will work together for good. God does not allow the righteous to be moved; our feet remain stable.

As we persevere through what can sometimes seem the darkest of circumstances, we do become stronger. It may be the last thing you feel is happening at the time but there comes a point when you look back and see how far you have come. So long as we allow Him, there is nothing that God cannot use to develop his character within us and make us strong and beautiful.

I used to get confused when I heard it preached about the importance of praising God regardless in times of trouble. I believe it is not a case of necessarily thanking God for the trouble, but for how he will carry us through the trouble and for what we will learn and how we will develop through the experience.

I have certainly experienced the power of praise in my life so far and how it really can feel like a "sacrifice" at times. I'm still learning to remember to regularly thank God for what is good in my life and for what he has done and what he will do. In all our lives there will be seasons of ease and seasons of hardship but throughout it all we need to keep praising God for who he is and what he has done.

To remain positive and strong through tough times is one of the best forms of witness to non Christians there is. Don't let your heart become hard or bitter as it benefits no-one.

I once heard it said that you cannot change your past but your past can change you. It can change you either for the better or for the worse. It all depends on how you view it. Your past can be like a rudder that guides you or it can be an anchor that hinders you, and at worst prevent you from walking in to the blessing God intended for you.

It is so important we leave the past behind us - all of it - our mistakes and our hurts. No looking in the rear view mirror as you could well miss something important ahead of you. We need to look at our future with faith and anchor ourselves in God and not our past.

When trials come in your life I urge you to press in deeper to God. Remember God sees the bigger picture of our lives from start to finish. He has all the pieces of the jigsaw and is carefully putting them together. Whatever apparent unrectifiable situations appear in your lives whether it be infertility, poor health, haemorrhaging finances or unsaved loved ones I encourage you .. NEVER GIVE UP!

Keep pressing in; keep persevering. Check yourself daily to ensure you are standing on God's word. God's word is truth and His promises are certain. God is always near. He is watching even when He seems to have turned His back and He is active when nothing seems to be changing. Remember God is working to perfect all that concerns you.

As you cling to God's word and learn to lean on and trust in Him you will see that your days become full of...

Hope and Laughter.